W9-CYN-039

Joe and Jude

A Memoir

Joseph Weiser

Printing by Falcon Books

San Ramon, California

ISBN 10: 0-9789312-0-3
ISBN 13: 978-0-9789312-0-9

PRINTED IN THE UNITED STATES OF AMERICA

Chapter One

The Beginning

The office was small. Nothing extreme, very ordinary. Just a small office with a jumbled desk, three aging chairs, and a wicker trash can. The walls were off-white and the floor concrete. A practical office. A business office. It was mid-afternoon and a thick beam of light shone through the lone window, illuminating the room with a soft glow. I stood for a moment in the doorway and watched the dust particles floating aimlessly in the light. One in particular caught my attention as it tarried on the edge before slipping off and disappearing completely into the relative darkness beyond the beam. *Ugh, how depressing*, I thought as I reached over and flipped on the switch, extinguishing the remaining particles in a barrage of artificial light. And that's when I saw it. Beneath the window. It had been shielded by the beam, but now with the overhead lamp blazing, it was as clear as anything I'd ever seen. A body. A head. Separated. Decapitated.

•

My story doesn't start with the broken body in my office, but neither does it end with it. But we'll get to that later. For now, it's back to the beginning. The story starts in Newark, New Jersey, with a five-year-old child who has just lost both parents to divorce. The marriage was a rough one and seemed doomed to fail from the start. My father, a truck driver, was married when I was born, though not to my mother. In fact, I didn't even meet him until he returned from the Army when I was about three or four. By this point, his first marriage had ended and he had since married my mother, but unbeknownst to him, my mother had been seeing someone while he was away. Even worse, the guy was in the Navy. When my father found out about this, a whole new war erupted on the home front and my parents were divorced by the time I was five. So I essentially gained and lost a father in less than two years. After the divorce, he effectively disappeared, the only reminder of his existence being the ten dollars a week I received for child support. My mother had custody of me, but now forced to work nights, she was almost as far gone as my father. Her job at a factory required her to work every day from three to midnight, meaning she left at two and got home at one. There was simply no way that she could properly care for me. In an effort to keep me off the streets and out of trouble, she sent me to my aunts' and uncles' houses. Now that's not poor punctuation there. My mother had twelve siblings, nine sisters and three brothers, and each day I would stay at one's house with his or her family. While we were very fortunate to be able to turn to such a large family in our time of need, it was far from an ideal situation. You see, my aunts, uncles, and cousins all had troubles of their own. No one in any of the families had money. Everyone was poor and everyone had problems. The last thing any of them needed was another mouth to feed, another face to wash, another spirit to nourish. But we were family, so I was welcome in their homes. At a price. Not one of the twelve was willing to take care of me for free. Not one. My father's ten dollars a week was my entrance fee. The monthly money would go directly to whichever house I was currently staying at, where it would be used for general housing costs and to purchase food for me. I was forced to carry around a thick, black magic marker with me at all times. When the food arrived at the house, I would give my aunt or uncle the pen and they would mark the food that was bought with the ten dollars in big black letters: **JOE.** And that's what I was allowed to eat. Labeled food. Joe food. There was no foraging in the fridge, no "Hey Mom, what's for dinner tonight"

I got what was labeled, what was mine. That's it.

At one point, I was sleeping on a cot on an aunt's screened-in porch. While certainly not the best situation, it was summer, so it wasn't really that bad. Besides, I didn't really understand that this, the porch, the marker, the cot, was bad. It was just life; it was just what I had to do. Looking back now it all seems absurd and wrong, but you don't question those kinds of things when you're a kid. You just live. I'd often lie there at night on the porch listening to the bugs as they tried to fight their way through the screen, desperately striving to reach the porch lamp, my inexhaustible nightlight. Listening to their audible battle, I empathized with their confusion, their desperate lunges toward the light. They too, it seemed, were reaching for something beyond their comprehension. If they could only reach that light, that source, then all would be illuminated, all would be clear. It was around this time that I first began to recognize my faith. Not religion exactly, just a spiritual awareness of something greater. But like the bugs, I was confused by it, overwhelmed, latching onto anything bright and hoping not to get fried. I was too young and had too little guidance to really get a hold on what I was feeling, but I knew I felt something. I also had a lot of other things to occupy my time, other things to worry about. For example, it was also around this time that I got peed on. My uncle, after a long bout with a whiskey bottle, had passed out on the couch inside. Awakening sometime in the night, more confused than me or the bugs, he began stumbling through the house in search of the bathroom. Eventually he found a door that opened, and, assuming that he'd opened the correct one, he proceeded to drop his trousers and let loose. Unfortunately, I awoke to a warm rain of urine that intermittently splashed my face and body, but worse my bed, my home. My uncle had no idea what was happening, even when I jumped up and retreated into the corner, wet and whimpering. He finished up, replaced his pants, and walked back inside. I stood for a while, stupefied, then lay down, huddled in the corner. I listened for the bugs, but couldn't hear them. Sticky and nauseated, I closed my eyes and fell asleep. The next day, I quietly washed my sheets, cleaned the bed, and kept the incident to myself.

When I was a freshman in high school, I had a crush on a girl. Jenny was her name. I really liked Jenny and finally decided to ask her out on a date. Unfortunately, dates cost money, which, as you now know, I did not have. So I decided to ask my uncle for the five dollars it would cost to go to the movies. Now this is obviously not an unusual situation. Most children haven't amassed much money of their own by this time in their life and often ask parents or guardians for a little help when it comes to such situations. But for me, it was different. I didn't get something like, "Sure, here you go, son. Good luck and when you get back we'll have a quick chat about the birds and the bees." It was, "Well, what do you have for collateral, Joe? If I'm gonna be lending you five dollars, I need something to hold on to 'til you pay me back. So what are you gonna give me?" This was a tough question for me to answer. I didn't have very many things of my own. As it turned out, the only thing I really had, other than my bat and glove which were not leaving my side, was an alarm clock. So off Jenny and I went to the movies and off the clock went to my uncle. Sadly, I never saw that clock again. It's pretty hard to pay off a five dollar debt when you are already going to school and working two jobs. All my money went to food and living costs; there was just never much left over. Sadly, it didn't last much longer with Jenny either. It was a fun night, but I guess she just wasn't impressed by my patched pants and oversized shirt. But such is life, such is love, such is high school.

I share stories like these because I want to give an accurate view of my childhood. That said, I don't hold a grudge against my relatives. They weren't evil people; they didn't beat or abuse me. Occasionally, things like the urination incident happened, but mostly my family was just poor; they had their own children to care for and worry about. I was an unwanted extra, an abandoned baby bird that slipped into another nest while the mother was out worm hunting. I wasn't theirs, but they couldn't turn down my feeble tweets, at least not while the ten dollars was coming in. But sadly, that wasn't always the case. Occasionally, my father would slip up, give in to his demons and neglect his financial duties, spending the ten dollars on booze instead. And that's when I'd have to pack up and move on to the next aunt or uncle's house and start the process all over again. As I said earlier, none of my relatives were willing to take care of me for free. Once the money stopped, all hell would break loose and I, tweeting and crying, would be tossed from the nest, abandoned all over again.

I can't complain too much, I suppose. After all, my basic needs were met. I was fed, housed, and my relatives provided me with an endless supply of hand-me-down clothing, which in hindsight, I am extremely grateful for. At the time, I didn't comprehend how much money this small generosity was saving my poor mother. All I knew was that every piece of clothing I "owned" was worn, ill-fitting, and often patched beyond belief. My essentially homeless situation and general raggedness were hard on me, especially during school. The school, by the way, was an unbelievable six miles from my cousins' houses; a distance that I had to travel by foot, in my too-big shoes, while other kids whizzed by on their bikes or in their parents' cars. This was, as I said, tough, but it wasn't bikes or fancy cars that I envied, it was families. Back in those days, all I could think about was being recognized as a person, instead of as a source of income. I wanted a normal family, a mother, a father, warm food for dinner. I wanted a permanent place with a room of my own. Nothing big, just a space that I could call my own, where I could have a little privacy and hang banners of my favorite baseball teams on the wall. But these things were an impossibility, a foolish dream, for they required money.

At this point, I feel it's fairly clear what an important role money, or the lack of it, played in my early life. The dollar bill was not only the key to success; it was your ticket to happiness, to a better life. As a result, I entered the work force at the absurdly young age of eight. My first job was delivering bread for a company called Hathaway Bakeries. I worked six days a week from 4:30 AM to 7:30 AM for four dollars a week. In the hours after work, I would walk the streets searching garbage cans and dumpsters for empty soda and beer bottles. Every day, my goal was to get twenty-five cents worth, the exact amount I needed to buy lunch at school. Looking back, it seems as though my entire childhood was split between fighting for survival and yearning for the familial normalcy that was so painfully apparent in the lives of my schoolmates.

High school, as I hinted earlier, was tough. It was during this time that I felt the most out of place. School just wasn't for me. I never liked it and with every passing day I felt more and more uneasy. As we all know, kids can be cruel, especially at that age. When you're fourteen, the last thing you want is to waltz into school with holes in your pants, tripping on your hand-me-down shoes. It certainly doesn't help to make friends. Fortunately for me, I was a good athlete. And again as we all know, athletes are the unofficial leaders of schools. They are the popular ones, the ones with power. It's not the teachers or the administrators who run the school, but the football players and the cheerleaders. That's just the way it works. Me? I was a baseball player. The best baseball player in the entire school. And it saved me. If you control a sport, it doesn't matter who you are or what you wear. As long as you keep smacking homers, you're golden. And that's exactly what I did. Come sophomore year, I made the varsity baseball team with little trouble. In a twenty-four game season, I hit nineteen home runs, crushing every record held in the county. As far as I know, that record still stands today. Baseball was my love, my life. Stepping out on the field was like stepping into a different world. One where money didn't matter, where you knew your position, your place. One where I had a team, a family. It was much more than a game to me. Swinging the bat, I felt free. Watching fans and teammates cheer as the ball cleared the fence, I felt loved, needed, comforted. And I worked to maintain this feeling, to prolong the illusion. All through my younger years, I lived with bat and ball in hand. During the summer months, I was out on the fields whenever I wasn't working. Whether it be a full pick-up game or just catch with a fellow addict, I was out there.

This obsession may well have saved me from a far crueler future. Had it not been for my love of baseball, I probably would have turned to a gang for support. When I was growing up in Newark, a gang represented each area of the city. The highlight of the evening was watching the dice games being played under the streetlights. As strange as it seems, watching these games under the lights was pretty alluring, almost magical at times. The dice aflame as they bounced along the sidewalk, the cheers, the jeers, the fights, the excitement of it all. Watching games from the various windows of my various relatives' houses, I caught a vicarious feeling of acceptance. Once again, my familial longings were manifesting themselves. I won't lie, gangs had, and I'm sure still have, a certain appeal. When you have nothing else, they start to look pretty good. They are, after all, families. Dysfunctional families, yes, but no more dysfunctional than my own. It was baseball and baseball alone that saved me from such a life.

Unfortunately, I failed baseball, failed my love. Money won out, as it often does in this world. After my record breaking season, I was contacted by recruiters for the New York Yankees. You can't imagine my excitement. It was the epitome of a dream come true. I was going to play for the Yankees. It was unbelievable! They offered me a spot on their triple A team, certainly an honor for someone as young as I was. But then they dropped the bomb. Compensation. They were only willing to offer me room and board for my efforts. "Unacceptable," I said. I needed an income, I needed money or at least that's what I thought. If only I'd had someone to guide or advise me, someone to explain what an amazing opportunity this was, that it didn't matter what they were paying me to start. But I didn't, I had no one. And as a result, I never really knew, never fully realized my true potential. As much as I loved baseball, it was the security and happiness of money that I truly craved. Once I had enough money everything would make sense, everything would come together. With this philosophy firmly in mind, I declined the offer and continued with life at school. At this point, I felt pretty depressed. It seemed as though my dreams had been dashed, as if what little wind had gathered in my sails had suddenly departed, leaving me stranded, powerless, at sea. And so, to the sea I went.

By the time I was sixteen, I'd had enough of high school and dropped out. My mother was still unavailable to me and my relatives had made it pretty clear that they had no further interest in housing me, so I began living at a Catholic house for boys. It wasn't an orphanage exactly, but more of a charity that took in kids whose parents could no longer care for them. It was certainly better than a porch cot. I stayed there for about five or six months, but as great as such institutions are, I never fully felt at home, which I think is the general consensus at such places. I was grateful to have a place to stay, but it wasn't home. It was a home, but not *my* home. I'd simply snuck into yet another nest. Often restless, I'd sit by the window and watch: people, cars, buses, whatever came by. One day I noticed a bunch of young men in Navy uniforms waiting on the corner for the bus back to Port Newark. Each day they were there waiting, their uniforms shining in the sun, girls staring and giggling as they passed by. Personally, I thought they looked pretty cool. And before I knew it I was once again being recruited. This time it didn't take much prompting. Dissatisfied with my current situation, I went down to the nearest recruiting post, lied about my age, and signed up. It's amazing how simple they made it. Back then all you had to do was fill out a form, sign your name, and off you went. They never checked to see if you were telling the truth. I guess they were just happy to get you, to get a new body. Once you signed up though, you had to take a bunch of aptitude tests. My scores were extremely high in many areas or at least high enough that they believed it when I told them, at sixteen, mind you, that I had not only graduated high school, but had completed two years of college as well. Ha! With those two years "completed," I was permitted to apply for flight training. Believe it or not, I was accepted to flight school, where, in reality, I received most of my education. And more importantly, I learned to fly jets. Pretty exciting stuff for a teenager, let me tell you. With no real connections holding me back, I threw myself into the Navy and ended up serving for nine years. During my time in, I caught the end of the Korean War and the beginning of Vietnam. I found much during this time, but I didn't find it, the *it* that had been evading me my entire life. There was brotherhood in the Navy certainly, but there wasn't family, there wasn't wholeness.

As you can imagine, a lot happened during this span of my life, but war is not what this story is about. I suppose it's about time I made clear what it really is about. So be it. It's about faith, about finding yourself, and about the help you can find along the way.

Chapter Two

A Whirlwind of Changes

As my tenure in the Navy came to a close, old feelings started rushing back. I had to fight off the feeling that I was being abandoned again. But after serving for nine years, I knew deep down that the Navy wasn't what I needed, that it wasn't what I was supposed to be doing, that it wasn't the family I was searching for. I'd been passing time and it had to stop. Unsure of what to do next or where to go, I found myself confused and uncertain as to where my destiny lay. And so I began to pray. Every day, I'd open my heart up to God, asking for guidance, for a sign that would lead me to where I was supposed to be. I needed to know what it was I was supposed to be doing. I pleaded for just the slightest direction, a hint as to why I am here. I wanted to know my destiny, or at least which road would lead me there. But my prayers, it seemed, were falling on deaf ears, so I went back to what I knew best: work.

I soon found myself at Morristown Airport teaching flying. My years flying jets in the Navy combined with my relatively charismatic personality made me a pretty successful instructor. I did quite well, if I do say so myself. But all in all, I still felt unsatisfied, as if I were missing something. I continued to pray, despite its apparent ineffectiveness. Unfulfilled, I decided to try something new. When off from work, I often found myself wandering through Seton Hall University. While walking through the campus, I would occasionally come across the ROTC students running, training, etc. As I watched, it seemed to me that they were somewhat uninspired, bored. Boring would probably be the worst word to describe my military experience; then again I was flying jets, so how bad could it have been? And then it hit me. These kids needed planes. I spoke with the ROTC and university leaders and before I knew it, I'd founded the first flight program in Seton Hall's history. The kids loved it and the program was a staggering success, but still I was unsatisfied. It didn't make sense. I was successful, I had money (at least more than I'd ever had before), but I still wasn't happy. The confusion weighed heavily on me. Uncertainty plagued me daily and I begged God to clear the mist surrounding my destiny, to reveal to me my purpose. But to no avail. I received no sign, no hint of enlightenment. No matter what I did, it just never seemed right, it never seemed to be what I was meant to do. And so, confused and depressed, I left Seton Hall University in hopes that my next venture would bring me some sort of peace and happiness.

While teaching at Morristown and later at Seton Hall, I spent a good amount of time at Belmont Park racetrack. The excitement of gambling was a draw, but what really hooked me were the horses themselves. They are such fantastic creatures, the embodiment of power and grace. The more time I spent there, the more I came to appreciate the business. Always ready to jump into something I know nothing about, I hurled myself into the fray and bought into a barn. It was a small stable, consisting of only six horses, three of my own and three owned by three separate owners. Watching your horses run a race, galloping as your trainers have taught them to, is an indescribable experience. But I wanted more. The horses were still too far from me. Sure I owned them, housed them, fed them, but I didn't know them. Enchanted, I decided to try my hand at training. So I took a weekend during the off-season and headed over to a farm in New Jersey. The next day I came home with a wild unbroken mare. The beauty of the beast was staggering. So much energy, so much spirit. I couldn't wait to begin.

It was the off-season, so I was able to take the horse to Belmont Park and begin her training. That first day, alone, standing on the track, I stared hard at the horse, picturing her galloping triumphantly around the track, wild mane flowing, dirt flying, crowds cheering. It was a beautiful vision for a beautiful day. I stepped closer, looked directly into the wild eyes of my horse and whispered, "I will break you."

Eight months later, it was done. She was ready for the races, literally champing at the bit. On a warm, breezy day, I led her and her jockey to their first starting gate. After a reassuring pat and a last proud look, I left them and headed for my seat. The gun cracked and my heart warmed with the sight of her streaking out of the gate. She was with them for most of the race, but gradually began to fall back. Ultimately, she finished last, but I felt a glorious feeling of accomplishment nevertheless. She'd run in and finished her first race. It could certainly have been worse. Besides, I also got paid. At 7 AM that morning, there were ten horses set to run in the race, but by post time four had been scratched for various reasons. Then, as I was walking to my seat after leading my horse down, another was scratched. Apparently, as the six remaining horses approached the starting gate, one unexpectedly threw its rider. I couldn't believe it. Since the track pays each of the top five, every horse was guaranteed a check, no matter where they finished. When we returned to the barn pseudo-victorious, everyone cheered and congratulated us. No one could believe my luck. It's terribly rare for someone with so little track experience and a new horse to get paid for his first race. It was truly a great day.

Later that night, I sat in my office alone. I should have been out celebrating, but I just couldn't shake the feeling that what I was doing was wrong, that I shouldn't be training horses. I prayed, once again asking for guidance, a sign. Not for the horse's water in the trough to part or for lightning to strike the weathervane, but for something, anything to give me the slightest hint as to what I should be doing. But alas, still nothing. No help; no sign. Though I was frustrated, my faith was not shaken. I figured there must be a reason God was holding things from me, a reason for my confusion, my bewilderment. So, attempting to be patient, I threw myself into my work, determined to be the best at what I was doing, no matter if it was my true life's work or not.

With my renewed ambition, the barn thrived. It was essentially a one man operation. I did the training, drove the truck, set up the races, and took the horses to the tracks and races they had the best chance of winning at. It was an exciting and successful time. Each of the horses in my barn did extremely well, except for one. A horse owned by a man named Sal Basile would, without fail, lose every race. Sal was a pretty entertaining character. At seventy, he was still a tall and imposing figure, probably about six three or six four. In a certain light, with his height, his scraggled white hair, and the slight bend to his back, he looked like a dark, aged undertaker; one who would creep up on you in the graveyard and whisper odd mumblings in your ear as you stood among the graves. It was a fitting image really because, in actuality, Sal *was* an undertaker. But his occasionally disconcerting appearance was instantly offset the moment he opened his mouth. Sal was the epitome of optimism. Throughout the years that I knew him, he was never once upset in my presence. And let me tell you, there are some pretty upset people at racetracks. But not Sal, he was always smiling, always the kind of guy that would find the one bright spot in an otherwise bleak and miserable situation. I suppose for an undertaker, such a disposition would be helpful, even necessary. Though his horse was truly terrible, Sal, the undertaker from Brooklyn, was fantastic. One day, he showed up at the barn, as he often did, to chat about his horse. The horse had just lost yet another race and I was beginning to feel pretty bad for old Sal. But as he rolled in, Sal seemed as jovial as ever. I laughed to myself as he stepped out of his car and quickly scurried around the other side to open the passenger door. Out of the door stepped a rather pretty woman who could not have been a day older than forty. *Sal, you scoundrel,* I thought. A thirty year difference. No wonder the old coot was grinning. I stepped up and shook his hand and he briefly introduced me to his lady friend before we walked towards the barn and his poor horse. As I said, I was disappointed in Sal's horse and felt bad about the continuous losses, but as we talked, Sal just shrugged and smiled. "She runs how she runs," he said and patted the horse's neck.

"But, Sal," I said, "she's come in last in every race she's run. Literally, every race. I'm sorry, I just don't know what else to try with her."

Sal just shrugged again, but his lady friend must have sensed how distraught I was, for she turned to me and said, "I've brought you something." Now, never having met this woman before, I was a little surprised and certainly intrigued. She reached into the folds of her coat and withdrew an unlabeled cardboard box. I looked at her questioningly, as she handed it over. "A gift," she said, looking me in the eyes. "Something to help you. With the horse, with everything."

"Well, thanks," I said, somewhat confused. Within the box was a large wad of tissue paper and within the tissue paper lay an eighteen inch clay statue and a small pamphlet. *Great*, I thought. *Just what I need. A statue.* Quite frankly, I was disappointed. For a moment there, when she'd looked at me, I thought maybe, just maybe she'd had something that could really help me. Not wanting to offend her, I tried not to let the disappointment show in my face.

"It's Saint Jude," she said, likely noting my confusion. She assured me that if I prayed to him, to Saint Jude, she was sure he would help me. I was unimpressed at best, but not wanting to seem rude I smiled and thanked her. After a couple more minutes of horse talk, Sal and his lady friend said their goodbyes and headed off, leaving me with the useless statue. Great. Not knowing or caring who Saint Jude was, my only concern was what to do with the statue. I walked back to my office and considered my options. I couldn't throw it out, as she was likely to come back at some point and would naturally want to know what I'd done with it, but I didn't want the stupid thing on my desk, where I'd have to stare at it all day. Looking around the office, I decided on the window sill that rested about eight feet above the concrete floor, thinking that it would be out of my way, but still visible if she walked in the door. Having found the statue a home, I quickly forgot about it and got back to work.

Things progressed normally for a while. I booked races, paid bills, fed horses, and essentially continued in my usual efficient yet uninspired fashion. But one morning about two weeks later, a change began. When I opened the door to my office on that particular day, nothing seemed out of the ordinary at first glance. Some dust particles floating through a beam of light briefly caught my eye, but other than that everything seemed pretty standard. It wasn't until I turned on the light that I saw it: the aforementioned headless body lying beneath the window. I walked over to inspect the body and see if I could figure out what had happened. As I peered closer, I recognized the face. It was Saint Jude. The statue had somehow fallen from the window and now lay broken, headless on the floor. I realize you may be feeling a little disappointed here, let down or deceived even, but let me assure you of something. That wrecked statue on that morning changed my life more than a true headless body possibly could have. Sure, there would have police inquiries and some misguided suspicions, but other than that it would have been no more than a lengthy inconvenience. But the fallen statue was something more, something not only symbolic, but something truly phenomenal. This may all seem a bit excessive, a bit far-fetched right now, but when you hear the rest you will understand.

My initial reaction was not this profound, but I was a bit upset or at least bothered to see it lying broken on the ground. It just didn't make any sense. The statue was made of clay and had fallen eight feet onto a concrete floor. It should have shattered or at least broken into several pieces, but instead it was neatly severed at the head. In addition, I couldn't for the life of me figure out how the thing had fallen in the first place. I had placed it firmly, solidly on the window sill. It had been in no danger of falling and it was still in place when I'd locked up the night before. But even if someone had been in the office, it was too high for anyone to have bumped into and the walls and window were sturdy enough not to shake much if someone bumped into them. And there certainly hadn't been an earthquake in the last twenty-four hours. So how could it have fallen? What could have caused it? Thoroughly perplexed, I gave up thinking about it. What was the point? I picked up the two pieces of Saint Jude and brought them over to my desk. I grabbed some glue and soon had the statue patched up. With its head securely refastened, I got up and placed it back on the window sill. I stood looking at it for a moment longer, but then shook my head, walked back to my desk, and got to work. By the next day, I'd pretty much forgotten about the incident.

One night about a week later, I found myself utterly depressed with my horses, my life, myself. It was the same old feelings, but intensified. Unable to sleep or concentrate on anything but my misery, I decided to go back to my office, in hopes of distracting myself and maybe even figuring out why my horses were losing so often recently. I opened the door and flipped the light switch. It was as if someone had rewound the earlier scene and was replaying it for their pleasure and my dismay. The only difference was the night sky outside the window. The statue lay in the same spot as before, the neck sliced in the exact same spot. I was completely unnerved. After staring for moment, I got really upset. I just didn't understand and the last thing I needed was more confusion, more uncertainty. I felt on the verge of a breakdown and found myself desperately trying to figure out how this eighteen inch statue could possibly have fallen eight feet and only have its head break off. Twice. It was absurd. Once again I picked it up off the ground and glued it back together. I replaced it on the sill and then returned to my desk. The panic had passed and I was now in a solemn and contemplative mood. I sat at my desk and stared off into space, just trying to relax and empty my mind. After a couple of minutes, I suddenly had an urge, for no reason whatsoever, to open my desk drawer. I pulled it open and lying there, staring up at me, was the little pamphlet that had accompanied the statue. I must have thrown it in there when I'd first received this strange gift.

This was all a bit overwhelming, a bit surreal, but what else was there to do at this point, but give in. I pulled the pamphlet out and began to read about The Life of the Forgotten Saint. This tiny booklet provided me with my first glimpse into the life of Saint Jude and in a moment I will give you yours, but first I want to dispel any doubts you may have concerning the fallen statue. I'm sure that given enough time you would be able to come up with some theory as to why the statue fell and why the only part that broke off was the head. Maybe the statue design was flawed and all the statues went out with weak necks. Or for you conspiracy theorists, maybe the company that manufactures them *intentionally* designed them with weak necks so that such accidents would be more likely to happen. Over the years, I've heard them all and quickly dismissed each as it came. For as the years passed and my friends became aware of my new belief in Saint Jude, I received many statues, of various designs, and every single one has somehow met with the same fate. For example, the statue that currently stands in my office was given to me by a friend several years back. That same evening I placed the statue on the dresser in my room and went out with my friend and a couple other guys. When I returned home, lo and behold, the statue was on the floor, beheaded, with no other sign of damage. I can only assume that my dogs, of which I have five, knocked into the dresser while playing. But nothing else had fallen and certainly nothing else had been decapitated. I will admit to you cynics that it is *possible* that these are all just a series of coincidences, but I can assure you that even the most cynical, the most doubting of you all, will at least be given pause after reading the remainder of my story and the miracles that take place within it. There sometimes comes a point where denying a miracle becomes more irrational than accepting it. So hold your tongues now, cynics, whilst I tell you of Saint Jude, the Forgotten Saint.

Chapter Three

The Life and Death of
Saint Jude Thaddeus

Because history about such men and such times can be rather long, rather taxing, and, at times, rather ambiguous, I will do my best to keep it short, to the point, and relevant. Saint Jude was son to Cleophas and Mary, wife of Cleophas, who was a cousin of the Virgin Mary. Cleophas was later said to have been murdered as a result of his unrelenting and outspoken devotion to and belief in the risen Jesus Christ. It is also written that, having grown up in the same area and possibly being related, Jude (as well as his brothers) and Jesus were likely close companions during their youth. Later on, Jude became one of the twelve apostles of Jesus and served him faithfully until his eventual death and martyrdom. During his time as an apostle, Saint Jude performed many miracles in the name of Jesus. One legend tells of The Cure of the King of Edessa. As the legend goes, King Abgar of

Edessa sent word to Jesus, begging that he visit him and cure him of leprosy. Unable to fulfill the request at that time, Jesus sent back word that he was unable to come, but would soon send someone in his stead. But the king was anxious, which I really can't blame him for, and in need of some immediate comfort. So he sent an artist to find Jesus and make a portrait of him. But upon seeing the face of the Lord, the artist was unable to complete the task. Pitying both the king and the humbled artist, Jesus pressed a cloth to his face and formed his image on it. Bearing the cloth, the artist then returned to the King, who was comforted and appeased by the gift. Later, after Jesus' ascension, Saint Jude visited Edessa and its king, as Christ had promised. He quickly healed Abgar of the disease and then, through his eloquent and moving portrayals of the Gospel, was able to convert not only the king and his family, but many of his subjects as well.

He performed other miracles, including the defeat of two Persian Magicians, but he was best known for his conversion work in Mesopotamia and Armenia. It's actually pretty interesting and inspiring stuff, but I will stick to my promise and keep this all as relevant as possible. Saint Jude fell out of fashion for a long period of time as a result of his name, Jude, being very similar to that of Judas, the traitor. People often confused the two, eventually causing Saint Jude to become known as the Forgotten Saint. In an attempt to rectify this, the church added his surname Thaddeus, meaning "generous and kind." These days, people who have been helped by Saint Jude often publish their thanks in newspapers in an attempt to raise awareness of his life and works. They work individually, yet collectively, to erase the Forgotten Saint's anonymity by sharing their stories with as many people as possible. There are prepared prayers that many such people use as guides for their interactions with Saint Jude, including ones for alcoholism, marital difficulty, mental sickness, financial aid, drug addiction, death of a loved one, and many more. Just to give you an example, here is one I found for a special request:

"St. Jude, glorious apostle, faithful servant and friend of Jesus, the name of the traitor has caused you to be forgotten by many. But the Church honors and invokes you universally as the patron of difficult and desperate cases. Pray for me who am so miserable. Make use, I implore you, of that particular privilege accorded to you to bring visible and speedy help where help was almost despaired of. Come to my assistance in this great time of need that I may receive the consolation and help of heaven in all my necessities, tribulations and sufferings, particularly — (*here you make your request*) — and that I may praise God with you and all the elect throughout all eternity. I promise you, O blessed Jude, to be ever mindful of this great favor. I will honor you as my special and powerful patron and encourage devotion to you."

I didn't use this particular prayer, or any other one for that matter, but just opened my heart and confessed my needs, my desires, hoping that someone would hear me and respond. Sal's lady friend physically gave me Saint Jude, but I believe that God, having heard my lifelong cries of despair, sent her, an unwitting messenger, to bring Saint Jude to my door. All those years I had thought no one was listening, but I merely had to be patient and wait, as King Abgar had. And now my wait was over. Saint Jude had arrived and the healing could finally begin.

In his New Testament letter, Saint Jude emphasizes that during difficult times the faithful should continue and persevere in the face of adversity, just as their forefathers had done before them. For this he has become the patron saint of desperate, lost, and impossible cases. As you surely know by now, lost is what I had felt my entire life. Lost, abandoned, and desperately confused. Thanks to Sal's young lady friend, I had finally been led to my savior. But of course it was not so simple as that. There's much more to come, much more to tell, miracles that, in my mind, rival those during his life as an apostle.

Now here I am almost glossing over the most important, or at least the most relevant, part of his history: his death. He died fearlessly, refusing to renounce Jesus and his beliefs and was thus granted martyrdom. Though impressive, it was not the martyrdom or his undaunted courage that caught my eye. What caused me to jump up in my chair was the way in which he was killed. My jaw dropped and with it the pamphlet, which after a brief flutter, came to rest at my feet. I couldn't believe it. Saint Jude had been beaten severely and was then, while still partially conscious, beheaded with an axe. I'll leave you to draw your own conclusions, but for me, there was no question. This was what I had been waiting for my entire life. While I couldn't yet see which way the arrow was pointing, I rejoiced in the fact that I could now at least see the signpost up ahead in the distance. As I sat there staring up at my window sill with newfound interest, I felt comforted for the first time in my life and knew with the utmost certainty that Saint Jude would no doubt become a major part of it.

Chapter 4

Ups and Downs

After the statue incident, my life continued on in essentially the same fashion as it had before. I still felt confused and uncertain of my path, but I at least felt like there was someone in my corner now, cheering me on. During this time of my life, I experienced a variety of ups and downs in both my business and personal life. In need of a change, I decided to leave off training horses. While training and racing were fun and profitable, there were certain aspects of the sport that were difficult to deal with on a daily basis. When you train a horse, you can't help but become close with it. The amount of time you spend working with a particular horse makes it more than just a piece of property. It becomes an individual, a companion, even an equal in some ways, for you rely on it just as much as it relies on you. And this is why I had to leave. During my training years, I had to put down six different horses. When you're as close with an animal as I've just described, it's as if you're ten years old and putting your beloved boyhood puppy to sleep. It's not like swatting a fly or squishing a spider, you're killing your friend, one of your closest companions. It's crushing, really, and at this point in my life, I'd been crushed enough.

So, as a result, I decided to remove myself from training and racing and concentrate instead on rehabilitation. And thus was born my horse therapy farm. It seemed to me that curing horses would inevitably be more rewarding then racing them. After all, it's racing that injures them in the first place. So naturally healing an animal you love will feel much better than endangering him. Excited by this new idea, I threw myself into the project. Before long, I had built the largest horse therapy farm on the East Coast from the ground up, complete with swimming pools, Jacuzzi tubs, two half-mile training tracks, and acres of turnout paddocks. The farm was an instant success and I was overrun with requests and reservations. People would come from all over to have their horses healed at my farm. Over the years, I rehabilitated some of the greatest horses in racing history. It was a beautiful, successful, and rewarding setup. But despite all this, I still couldn't shake the feeling that this wasn't what I was supposed to be doing. Once again it struck home just how wrong I'd been as a child. Money, which I had more of now than ever before, did not make happiness, did not bring peace. It could cause distraction through temporary satisfaction, but overall it was merely a form of appeasement. Though your senses may be gladdened by fancy cars and lavish living, your soul remains lost and unfulfilled. Money was a means to an end that was neither what I wanted nor where I wanted to be. Yet there I was.

During the late eighties, President Ronald Reagan suddenly changed a bunch of tax laws that drastically affected the racing industry. The glory days of racing were over and everyone felt the repercussions. With my farm being one of the largest in the country, we were hit worse than most. Less money was floating around so people in the business no longer wanted to spend the kind of cash required to rehabilitate a horse. It simply wasn't worth it. I held out for a while, but things continued to get worse and the business plummeted. Nearly bankrupt, I was forced to consider other options. I decided to restructure the farm into a riding school for the handicapped, but with dwindling funds, I was unable to keep the property, which left me with thirty horses and nowhere to house them. With most of my remaining money, I purchased a place in Old Westbury on Jericho Turnpike. It is here that I opened the riding therapy school for the handicapped. This move was truly one of the most rewarding of my life. Helping children to overcome their fears and gain new hopes was a moving experience. After only one year of operation, I started and hosted the first Special Olympics in the state of New York. We ran a fantastic program and this was our way of sharing it with everyone. It was so successful and gratifying that we held it the next year as well. Yet even with all these accomplishments and personal rewards, I still felt that something was missing. In addition to this old feeling, my job was mainly administrative. I was constantly cooped up in my office doing paperwork, while others, professional riders, worked with the kids and horses. I missed the personal interactions; I missed getting my hands dirty. Money was also pretty tight at this point. While the therapy farm was a cultural and spiritual success, it wasn't nearly lucrative enough to support such a large farm. As the saying goes, never invest in something that eats.

One day, while I was sitting in my office pondering my current situation, it occurred to me that I needed some new supplies for the farm. So I hopped in the car and headed towards a hardware store in Old Westbury. As I was driving down Hallowed Lane, the service road to the Long Island Expressway, and just easing around a bend in the road, two cars suddenly slammed into one another. I hit the brakes and jumped out to see what I could do. The crash was terrible. Both cars were totaled and two people were quickly declared dead. Since I was a witness to the scene, the police had to take my statement. I told them what I'd seen and was soon on my way. Though certainly sad and upsetting, the incident promptly migrated to the back of my brain. My part in it was over, so why dwell on it?

About a week and a half later, a wiry little man showed up at the farm looking for me. He was shown into my office and introduced himself as an investigator from an insurance company. He had seen the report I'd given the police, but his company needed a statement as well. So I again recounted what I'd seen. No big deal. He was a nice little guy and after the interview we got to talking about ourselves and what we did. I gave him a quick tour of the farm and explained about the Navy, the flying, the old farm, the new one, the horses, the handicapped kids, etc. And then he left. It was a nice exchange, an interesting conversation, I suppose, but certainly nothing extraordinary or particularly groundbreaking. But about two weeks after that, he showed up again one Saturday afternoon. This struck me as a little odd, but after some brief small talk, he explained why he'd come. He was on his way to the marina where he kept his boat and was wondering if I'd take a ride over there with him. With all my work for the day finished, I agreed. As we drove over, he explained the situation. The marina was in foreclosure and was, as a result, being run by a court appointed receiver. Apparently the receiver was in over his head. My newly acquired friend had very little confidence in the man's ability to run the marina and was naturally concerned about his boat. He'd brought me along, figuring that with my experience in the Navy, I probably knew something about boats.

That day was November 25th, 1996. I will forever remember the date, for it was the first day in my life that I felt like I belonged. From the moment I stepped out of the car and into the marina, I felt at home. It's hard to describe; it just felt right, like when you pull on a sock that's exactly the right size. Perfection.

All through my young adult life, especially during my years in the Navy, I'd had a love for the water and boats. I'd often wondered what it would be like to own a marina, never thinking that the opportunity would actually present itself. This was where I was supposed to be. I finally knew it. During the visit and immediately after, I gathered as much information about the place as I could. I can't explain why I thought this all might work. It doesn't really make any sense. I was dead broke. The last of my money had gone into the handicapped farm and that was essentially through. I barely had enough money for lunch, let alone to buy a marina. But ignoring logic and common sense, I probed further and contacted the bank that was doing the foreclosure. Acting like I had money, I asked them what it would take to purchase the marina. They informed me that if I were to buy the marina, the bank would oversee the sale, but I first had to do business with the present owners, as the foreclosure had not yet taken place and legally the current owners still owned the property. The foreclosure was set for December 17th of the same year, which didn't leave me with much time. I thanked the bank, contacted the owners, and planned a meeting to discuss the sale of the marina.

A couple days later, I traveled to Connecticut where the owners lived, discussed the purchase, and made my offer. They informed me that the bank wanted $1,550,000.00 plus $850,000.00 in back taxes, both of which I agreed to, despite having essentially no money to my name. I insisted on terms that would give me time to raise the money, meaning that I wanted to move the closing date from December 17th to some time during February. To my delight, and amazement really, they agreed. As a good faith deposit, I wrote them a check for $10,000.00; however, I told them not to deposit it until the contracts were drawn up and signed. We shook hands and I drove home elated, ecstatic, electrified. I could barely contain my excitement. Finally, things were beginning to feel right. But unbeknownst to me, the owners had to get the bank's approval before they could sign the contracts.

The bank called me the next day and flat out declined my terms. They were set on the original foreclosure date of December 17th and refused to wait until February to close. The only way that they would agree was if I could put down fifteen percent and close by the year's end. Fifteen percent? Are you kidding me? That's $232,500.00. I almost dropped the phone. It was insane; at this point I had maybe $50.00 to my name. How in the world was I going to raise that much money in less than a month, not to mention how I was going to get financing for the full amount by two weeks after that? It was impossible. I told the bank that it just wasn't possible to get a mortgage in less than a month, especially when that month was filled with Christmas and New Year's. I didn't dare tell them that I didn't have the down payment money. It was best to just let them assume that if they could accommodate me a little, then everything else would go smoothly. My plan seemed to work, as they told me not to worry about a mortgage right away. If I qualified, they would give me interim financing until I could get my own mortgage, so all I had to do was come up with the $232,500.00 deposit. Once again, I quickly agreed, despite being at a complete loss as to how I was going to acquire this money.

Every day and every night from that conversation onward, I prayed to Saint Jude Thaddeus, hoping against hope that he would hear my pleading words. There had to be a way, if only he would lead me to it. This certainly qualified as a desperate, impossible cause. If this deal didn't go through, I'd go bankrupt. I needed to get that money. While I had no real plan, other than excessive prayer, I proceeded as though I did, hoping to fool everyone, including myself, into thinking that I actually knew what I was doing.

Step One: I scheduled another meeting in Connecticut with the owners and their lawyer. If I could stall for a little longer, I'd still have a chance. Playing as a nervous potential buyer, I explained to them that everything was happening too fast for me. I needed time to think about things and get the down payment together. They understood my concerns, but insisted that I at least give them the down payment check. I agreed as long as they promised not to deposit it until I had all the funds in the bank. Unbeknownst to them, that same bank account currently read something in the area of $82. The attorney, at the risk of losing his license, agreed, saying that he would hold the check in his desk until I told him to deposit it. So I handed it over and he stamped the back FOR DEPOSIT ONLY, explaining to me that he would send the bank a copy of the front and back, thus buying us some time. I thanked them profusely, but was careful not to overdo it. Exuberant praise might have made them suspicious.

Step Two: Qualifying for the mortgage. With the help of the owners' lawyer, I'd managed to stave off the wolves for a while, but there was still a lot that needed to be done, the most important of which was qualifying for the bank's interim financing. I had just come through some pretty tough financial times and my credit report was not what one would call stellar, or even good, for that matter. Only two months earlier, I'd been turned down for a $1,000.00 limit credit card. There was no way I'd be approved for a two million dollar mortgage. Things were not looking good. I started to panic. The jig was up; I was done for. And so I prayed and prayed again. I needed Saint Jude now more than ever. The prayers calmed me. I'd felt his presence through all the proceedings to date. I just couldn't believe that he'd let me down now. I was nervous, for sure, but I kept my faith.

The foreclosing bank uses a New Jersey based company called T.R.W. to investigate their customers' credit. Despite my faith, I thought I was screwed. There was just no conceivable way that this would work. When I got a call from my attorney the next day, I was visibly sweating. I set myself up for disappointment and had already begun to despair when he said four simple words that changed my life and cemented my faith in Saint Jude: "The bank approved you." What? I couldn't believe what I heard; it was inconceivable. I almost fainted from pure disbelief. After a couple of stunned seconds, I managed to squeak out a question.

"But how? What did they say about my credit?" I was incredulous and I think he knew it.

He laughed and did his best to explain. Apparently T.R.W. was in the process of moving to Texas. All their computers and credit checking devices were on trucks on the way to Texas. So my credit report had come up not as bad, poor, terrible credit, but as simply no credit. As far as the bank knew, I had no credit history whatsoever, which is certainly better than bad credit, but it's still not good. I couldn't believe that they would approve someone with no credit. I asked my attorney how this was even possible. He said the bank had decided that a person didn't need credit as long as he had money. Once again, I was shocked. That kind of thinking at a bank? It was such an unorthodox bank response that I almost accused my attorney of playing some sort of mean trick on me. But believe it or not, it was true. I'd been approved. To say that I was excited would be a vast understatement. It seemed like Saint Jude was simply removing any obstacle that stood in my path. I had never been more certain of his presence, of his assistance.

Step Three: Finding the down payment money. With the mortgage no longer barring my path, the only obstacle left was the down payment money. I only needed that $232,500.00 and the marina would be mine. But what a ridiculous amount of money to raise in a month. It was absurd, but it had to happen; it just had to. I applied for loans, but was turned away by every bank I approached. So I just started talking to people, to everyone I knew. Bargaining, promising, begging. Everyone said that they would love to help me, but it just wasn't possible. I was on my own. Desperate, I even tried organized crime. As a result of my rough childhood and my long involvement in horse racing, I knew a fair amount of shady characters. Using these contacts, I was able to get in touch with even shadier folks, namely loan sharks and mob bosses. But even they turned me down, convinced that I'd never be able to pay them back. It was hopeless.

Meanwhile, the attorney holding my deposit check was getting antsy. We were nearing the end of the year and he was reaching his breaking point. He kept calling me, telling me to get my affairs in order because if he waited any longer to deposit the check, he risked being accused of fraud. I begged him to be patient, to give me a couple more days. He agreed, but I was still sweating. From here, things looked pretty bleak. Not only was the deal not going to go through, but I was about to bounce a $200,000.00 check. Then, to make matters worse, the owners got another offer. Jack Brewer, a real bigwig in the industry, who owns nineteen marinas, suddenly expressed an interest in purchasing. As if I needed any more pressure. To a small time guy like me, Jack Brewer was a Goliath. And this little David was currently running around with no slingshot. There was just no way to beat a man like that, not without divine intervention anyway. In order to even stand a chance, I had to sign the contract of sale. So on December 13th, 1996, I signed, which left only seventeen days to hand over the down payment and close the deal. For this sale to take place, nothing could go wrong; every step had to be ascended flawlessly.

Once again, I began to pray to Saint Jude Thaddeus. As I mentioned earlier, Saint Jude is often referred to as the Forgotten Saint. As the two Apostles have very similar names, the lines between Jude the martyr and Judas the traitor are often blurred. Preferring not to think about Judas and the evil that took place, humanity intentionally overlooks and avoids the topic. And lost in the traitor's shadow is the pious Saint Jude, ignored and forgotten. As for me, I knew that there was no one else I could turn to; no human could give me the help I needed. And so I made a promise. If he would help me, as he had been doing all along, then, as a show of my gratitude, I would name the marina after him. I then vowed to spend the rest of my life making sure that his name was never forgotten again. It was December 27th, which left me with only four more days. I could only hope that the attorney holding my check hadn't deposited it yet.

The next morning I awoke with an idea. I figured I may as well go down to the foreclosing bank and talk to the person handling the sale. Maybe I could figure out some way to delay the process. On my way there that afternoon, I thought about everything that had happened. I couldn't believe that this had all happened merely because I'd randomly witnessed a car accident, because I'd briefly mentioned to the insurance investigator that I was in the Navy. And then it hit me. We'd gone to the marina that day because the investigator was worried about his boat, worried about the status of the marina under the care of the court appointed receiver. I'd fallen so hard for the marina that first day that I'd neglected to notice all the problems. The place was falling apart. And then I remembered something else. It was all coming at me so fast now. There was still a chance. A while back, I'd looked over the marina's books and noticed that the receiver, in an effort to keep the business going, had spent all the proceeds he'd received in advance for the 1997 year. Interesting, this could work. When I got to the bank I was exhilarated, but I had to be calm, hide my excitement, and play this just right. I took a deep breath, went in, shook the woman's hand, and began to explain.

I laid out a three point argument, followed by a pointed and hopeful solution.

Point One — I had looked around the marina and noticed that it was in desperate need of repairs. The marina, if left as it was, could be considered extremely dangerous. Owning an unsafe establishment was out of the question.

Point Two — The court appointed receiver had shirked his duties, which was why the marina was so hazardous to begin with. And then, to make matters worse, he had used up all the advance proceeds for 1997.

Point Three — With little to no money coming in for the '97 year, there was no way that I could afford the repairs necessary to turn the marina back into a safe haven. Something had to be done.

Pointed and Hopeful Solution — Without question, I needed some working capital to run the marina and, more importantly, to make it safe. So it seemed logical that the deposit money, $232,500.00, being held by the unbelievably patient attorney should be released to me for the purpose of working capital.

When my argument was complete, the banker was noticeably, and understandably, upset. She immediately called the receiver to verify what I'd told her. He admitted that there was no money to hand over to me, claiming that he'd had to spend the money to keep the business going. She hung up the phone, her face ashen, and sighed in what I interpreted as a combination of disbelief and dismay.

"I can't believe this has been happening and no one knew about it," she said. "This is crazy."

I nodded, too nervous to speak.

"You'll have to take out a second loan, you know," she continued.

I nodded again.

"Do you have anything that could be used as collateral? A house or a car maybe?"

At that, I almost lost my voice completely. Collateral? Please, I could barely afford dinner. But I had to say something.

"I have a horse," I said, barely breathing.

"A horse?"

"Yeah, I'm a trainer. And rehabilitator."

"I see. Well, I have to run this by our attorneys first."

This was trouble. The horse, the only one remaining of the thirty I used to have, was thirteen years old and was, at best, worth $500.00. She picked up the phone and I held my breath, my face even more ashen than hers. I listened as she explained the situation. It all just sounded so absurd. I thought for sure that this was it, the end of the ride. After a couple minutes she hung up and turned back to me.

"Okay," she said, "he's going to call the Jockey Club to see about putting a lien on a horse and then call me back. Then we'll make our decision and let you know."

"Sounds great," I said, trying to look as unconcerned as possible.

"Thanks for coming in, Mr. Weiser. We'll be in touch." We shook hands and I got out of there as quickly as possible. I couldn't believe that neither she nor the attorney had thought to ask the value of the horse and I didn't want to be around if it happened to occur to them. The only reason I can come up with is that the attorney just assumed that the bank had already approved of the value and only needed to know if they could use it as collateral. As for the banker, my guess is that she either knew nothing about horses and was too embarrassed to ask or, with all the confusion and craziness, she just plain forgot. Either way, it was an enormous bit of "luck." I went home, ate some dinner, thanked Saint Jude for all his help, and went to sleep. The next day I got a call from the bank officer, letting me know that they had approved my second loan. I immediately called the lawyer holding my check and told him what had happened. He almost fainted in disbelief, but recovering, he congratulated me on being the new owner of the marina. The next day I had the name officially changed to The Jude Thaddeus Glen Cove Marina, in honor of the man who had made it all possible.

Chapter Five

Feeding the Marina

The actual closing for the marina took place on December 31st, 1996, the last possible day. It lasted most of the day, starting at ten in the morning and not ending until about four-thirty in the afternoon. When everything was finally complete, I sat back in my chair and let out a heartfelt sigh of relief, gratitude, and disbelief. I had just closed on a two million dollar piece of property without a penny crossing the table. I was in shock. A warm, happy, ecstatic state of shock.

I reported for work the next day, New Year's, just as pleased with myself and the situation as the night before. I thought the hard part was over, but man, was I wrong. By the end of the day, my smile had disappeared and I was all business. I'd come to realize that this was just the beginning. I may have grabbed a life vest, but I was still in a sinking ship. I was still broke and had no income to look forward to for the 1997 season. There was a bright spot though. At this time there was a local

program in effect that called for the revitalization of the Glen
Cove waterfront. The marina, now called The Jude Thaddeus
Glen Cove Marina, was a major part of the plan. The Mayor of
Glen Cove started to frequent the marina, asking questions and
making suggestions. He was a real nice guy and he helped me as
much as he could, taking me around and introducing me to
bankers, members of the SBA, and other influential people. I
soon learned that there was a lot of low interest money available
through this waterfront revitalization project; however, when I
applied for it, I was quickly denied. Apparently, I didn't have
enough experience in the marina field to qualify. Though frus-
trating, it was true, so how upset could I really get? This was certainly a disappointment though and another soon followed.
Going over all the files and paperwork in my office, I came
across a massive amount of outstanding tax liens. It seemed that
they had been purchased by a man from Glen Cove. Buying up
liens was his business apparently, and my new marina owed
him a lot. The debt was currently at approximately $825,000.00,
which he was collecting twenty percent interest on. I panicked
briefly when I realized that he could foreclose at any time. I
called him and set up a meeting to discuss the debt. Thankfully,
the meeting went smoothly. He told me not to worry, that I
could have all the time I needed. A nice gesture for sure, but
then again he was making twenty percent. It was certainly a
lucky break though. *Another* lucky break. Somehow every obstacle that threatened to knock me out of business and end the

dream was being held at bay, dissipating before my very eyes. But others still remained and I prayed that Saint Jude would stay with me.

The next problem was an anticipated one, but that certainly didn't make it any easier to deal with. My interim mortgage was only for three months, so I had to find a bank that would be willing to give me a real mortgage. Not an easy task, for sure. While working hard at repairing and rebuilding the marina, I applied to every bank I could find in hopes that one would be willing to give me a chance. They were not willing, to say the least. Every bank turned me down, as they very well should have. After all, my only real collateral was a thirteen-year-old horse. I couldn't really expect to slip by on that one again. In desperation, I went back to the interim bank and asked for more time. Thankfully, they agreed to add on another three months. And then another three months, and another, and another. In total, they rolled my mortgage over four times in three month chunks, equaling over a year of interim mortgaging. Despite this unexpected help, money was really getting tight. I was bailing hard, but the ship was still sinking. Every night, while lying in bed, I continued to ask Saint Jude for help. I was having trouble thinking straight. The fact that the odds were always stacked against me was really starting to get to me. There was no money coming in and I desperately needed a mortgage. Each day flew by, every passing hour bringing me that much closer to bankruptcy and failure.

One day, while sitting at my computer and going over the accounts receivable, I came across something that gave me a little hope. The one thing I had going for me was that a lot of people owed the marina, and therefore me, money. But most of the debtors owed very little, mere pocket change slipping through holes in the marina's patched pants. I called and hassled many of these small timers, but on this day I came across the main offender. This one guy owed over $4,000.00. Scoring that money would be a big step towards buying the marina a brand new pair of slacks. I called and left him a message, hoping that he would just come forward, apologize, and hand over the money. And then I called several more times. Naturally, I didn't hear back from him for over two weeks, but finally I got a call. He threw a fit when I unapologetically told him to pay up. According to him, the marina owed him money. Apparently, the previous owners had ripped him off. This annoyed me a bit. I explained that the old owners were gone and that his little squabble had nothing to do with me. He could either pay me the money, in full, or I would sell his boat. It was as simple as that. At this affront, he hung up. I waited two weeks or so and then called back, but he refused to take my calls. At this point I had no other option but to contact the Sheriff's department. He did owe me money after all, and I really needed it. Whatever had happened between him and the prior owners was not my fault, not my problem. My problem was money and his debt was a big part of the solution. The Sheriff sent papers notifying him that a lien had been placed on his boat and if the debt remained unpaid, the boat would be sold at a public auction in thirty days time.

I got a call the second after he received the papers. As soon as I picked up the phone he began screaming, telling me I couldn't sell his boat. After about five minutes or so, he calmed down and the verbal barrage ceased. He apologized for yelling and admitted that it wasn't my fault that the previous owners had screwed him. He wanted to come in and show me how badly he'd been ripped off.

"Look," he said, now calm and rational, "don't sell the boat. I know you are owed money. I understand that, but I paid the marina, up front, to repair my boat. They took the money, stole the money, and never repaired a thing. My boat is a wreck. Now does that seem fair to you?"

"Of course not," I replied, "but that has nothing to do with me. That's between you and them."

"Maybe we can help each other," he said.

"The only way you can help me is by paying your bill." That didn't go over well. The phone was silent for a minute. I could almost see him fuming over the phone, but he kept his cool and finally spoke.

"Okay, but please be patient. I want to show you how badly they screwed me. I'll come out there next weekend and we can discuss this face to face."

I agreed and true to his word, he showed up that Sunday. He took me to his boat and calmly explained what had happened. It was true; his boat was looking pretty bad. I sympathized with his story, but insisted that he pay his bill. Then, in response, I calmly explained my situation and made it painfully clear how badly I needed the money. Something in his expression changed as I spoke. When I'd finished, he thought for a moment and then started asking me all kinds of questions. Who was giving me interim financing, how much did the marina owe, how long was I covered for, etc., etc.

"Wait, wait, wait," I said. "Where are you going with this?"

He smiled at me for the first time and replied, "I'm a loan officer. I work for a bank called China Trust and believe it or not, we've been looking to finance waterfront property on the North Shore of the island. Now that I think about it, the marina would be perfect. Maybe we can help each other after all."

I almost fainted with shock. A loan officer. This guy, this random person I had picked from a computer full of debtors, was a loan officer. I couldn't believe it. Thank you, Saint Jude! Within two weeks this man had a commitment letter for me and within two months I had closed on a new mortgage. Unbelievable. I have to admit, it wasn't the best mortgage in the world, but it was a mortgage and that's all I needed at this point. It was only a three year mortgage, with the bank having the option to renew. Also the interest rates were very high, with stiff penalties if you were late. But, like I said, it was a mortgage and it allowed me to pay off my interim mortgage, as well as the lien gatherer that was now holding $885,000.00 worth of tax liens. For the first time in ten years, the marina was free of debt. All bills were paid and everything was up to date, but more importantly, I knew that Saint Jude was there with me and that he was in full support of the Jude Thaddeus Glen Cove Marina.

With the mortgage out of the way, I'd plugged the biggest hole; the ship was beginning to level out. Now all I had to do was keep from springing any more leaks. It was time to see if I could actually make the business work. Several others before me had failed and, as the Glen Cove Waterfront Revitalization Project was so quick to point out, I had very little marina experience. Much to my surprise, the boaters rallied behind me, wanting the marina to succeed. Many of them even offered to pay a year in advance just to give me some capital to work with. So with a little bit of money and a lot of support, I started to make changes. By the time my second season came to an end, I had built Glen Cove's first and only waterfront restaurant, installed 2400 feet of new bulkheading at a cost of $475.00 per foot, reconfigured the slips to host 367 boats instead of the 125 it had supported before, and had begun storing 700 boats over the winter instead of the former 215. The restaurant, Steamboat Landing, fast became one of the biggest hot spots on the North Shore of Long Island and the slips filled up even faster than I'd hoped. The business was beginning to thrive and for the first time in my life I was content. I felt good about the accomplishments, but I felt even better about the fact that whenever someone mentioned the marina, they spoke Jude Thaddeus' name. Most of the boaters knew about him by now, and those that didn't quickly learned who he was. The word was spreading and with each passing day he became less and less the Forgotten Saint.

Chapter Six

The Final Miracle

With my mind finally at ease about the business, there was only one thing that was bothering me: I owned a marina, but I didn't own a boat. Back in the eighties, I had bought a 45-foot Bayliner. It was a beautiful boat and, as I mentioned earlier, I've always loved boats and the water. But when the horse business went bad I was forced to sell it. Unfortunately, at the time of the sale I still owed $140,000.00 on it and was only able to sell it for $115,000.00, leaving me $25,000.00 short. As a result, I had to pay this remainder over a period of five years. This procedure is known as a voluntary repossession, which goes on your credit report. With this history, I was unable to get financing for another boat. I kept trying though, but was continuously turned down. I refused to give up.

One night, as I sat browsing the internet for boats for sale, I stumbled across a 45 foot Bayliner. Memories of my old boat came rushing back and my desire for a boat doubled. It was being sold by a company accurately, but unimaginatively named Staten Island Boat Sales. After viewing the site, I was so nostalgic that the next morning I took the hour and a half ride to Staten Island just to see her. Seeing me studying the Bayliner, the salesman ambled up and informed me in a conspiratorial voice that the boat was old and tired. What I needed, he said, was a Carver. He brought me over to the other side of the room and introduced me to a magnificent 53-foot Carver. She was beautiful beyond belief. Within a few minutes, I was filling out a credit application form. In hindsight, I'm really impressed with that salesman's selling skills. I left a small deposit and headed back to the marina. As I entered my office, only an hour and a half later, the phone was ringing. It was the salesman . . . telling me I'd been turned down.

I was furious. It just didn't make sense to me. Twenty years ago I couldn't afford a boat and had no trouble getting financing. Yet now, I was the owner of an extremely successful marina, but no one would even think about giving me financing. That same evening, while in bed, I spoke aloud to Saint Jude and explained my feelings and begged for his intervention. I promised that if he could find it in his heart to help me get the financing I needed, I would name the boat after his mother. My prayer complete, I fell into a deep, comfortable sleep. Nothing out of the ordinary happened for a while, but about ten days later, on a rainy Sunday afternoon, I was sitting at my desk staring off into space when a distress call came over the ship to shore radio. It was something about a captain whose boat had lost power in both engines, but I wasn't really listening. About five minutes later, the same distress call was repeated. This pattern continued for about twenty minutes. I couldn't understand why no one was responding. Both the Coast Guard and the Nassau Police patrol those waters. Strange. I couldn't just leave him there, so I called back over the radio and got the captain's position. It was about ten miles away. A couple minutes later, I set out in the marina workboat to find him.

It took a while, but I eventually found him. When I arrived, the boat, drifting, was being tossed about by the small storm. The captain, wet and harried, yelled his thanks and threw me a line. I towed him all the way back to the marina, where he thanked me profusely and asked me to repair the boat. Then he hopped in a cab, told me he'd be back in a couple days, and drove off. The repairs turned out to be pretty simple. Both engines were low on oil and had automatically shut off in order to protect themselves. When the captain returned, dry and a good deal happier, I briefly explained the situation. He told me that he didn't know the boat well; he'd only been hired to deliver it. I nodded and he took the bill, asking if the owner could just send me a check. I agreed and off he went again.

About three or four days later, I got a call from the owner. He couldn't thank me enough and told me all about the boat. As it turned out, it was being traded in on a new boat and the captain had been hired to deliver it to the dealer. And to what dealer was it headed? Why to none other than the aptly named Staten Island Boat Sales, the very same dealer that had just turned me down. When the boat finally reached its destination, the owner of Staten Island Boat Sales was so grateful that he personally called me up to thank me, saying that if there was anything he could ever do for me, I need only ask. So ask I did. I told him about the 53-foot Carver I'd gotten turned down for and he asked me to give him a couple days and he would get back to me. The very next day, he called me back and said, "If you want the boat, just come down and sign the papers. I got you approved. Thanks again for all your help." A week later, the boat was at the Jude Thaddeus Glen Cove Marina with its new name painted on back: Mary of Cleophas. I had kept my promise and now Saint Jude and his mother were reunited.

Chapter Seven

Parting Thoughts

I am sure that over the next few years I will be able to write several more chapters on the miracles of Jude Thaddeus, but until then, I would like to leave you with these parting thoughts. I started out as nothing, a poor child who had no place he could call home. Throughout my life, I jumped from job to job, just as I'd gone from relative to relative as a child, all along searching for meaning and purpose. Imagine a man, dead broke, trying to purchase a marina that cost over $2,000,000.00 plus another $2,000,000.00 in repairs. Why would he continue against all logic and reason, with no hope of achieving his goal? It's absurd.

Imagine a bank throwing normal procedure out the window, as it financed a man with no credit. It's crazy.

Imagine a lawyer, a professional bank attorney, just assuming that a bank did its homework on the value of a horse as collateral and then advising financing. It's ridiculous.

Imagine the same bank giving a second loan to cover a deposit that never existed to a person who still had no credit. It's nuts.

Imagine another lawyer who risked his license, his career, to help someone he didn't even know by holding an escrow check in his desk long past the time when it should have been deposited. It's insane.

As unlikely as each scenario was, they all came together to allow that one man to overcome the odds and close on the unobtainable marina. Yet still ahead were more challenges, just as seemingly insurmountable as the others. A mortgage was still needed and out of ninety debtors, the man randomly picks the one customer who happens to be a loan officer, who works for a company that is looking to finance waterfront property. And then this debtor, who was threatened and upset, takes it upon himself to loan the man $2000.00 to help cover costs.

And what about the broken down captain, whose distress call no one else would answer. Where was the Coast Guard? Where were the police? Both patrol the waters, but were mysteriously absent. And this captain just happens to be delivering a boat to the same dealer that had just rebuffed the man. Then the owner, of his own volition, goes out on a limb to pressure a bank to loan money to a man with terrible credit.

It all seems a little strange, a little unlikely. Unfathomable even. How could this one man have been so lucky as to overcome such insurmountable odds? Well, I think we all know by now, that he certainly didn't do it all on his own. But he did have the most important thing: faith. There's a lot to think about in my story, a story about faith, hope, and miracles; a story that ranges from poverty to planes, from horses to baseball, from boats to holy men. Some very remarkable things took place and they all began when Saint Jude Thaddeus let me know, on that fateful day, that he wanted my help. The many statues, beginning with the first one in my office, that have somehow been decapitated have changed my life. Some may call it coincidence and some may call it luck, but I call it divine intervention. In today's world, scientists are always trying to give a scientific explanation for everything that happens. It's all facts and no heart. Well, there's no place for science in my story, nor is there any room for luck or coincidence. Throughout my life, even when things seemed hopeless and bleak, I believed. I never lost hope and I always had faith. The miracles that took place during my life were asked for, prayed for. They were prayers that could only have been granted by Saint Jude Thaddeus, the lover of lost causes and impossible cases. I am certain that if I could see his face, he would be smiling and quite pleased with the work he's done. For his help and his kindness, I am, and will always be, forever grateful. He has been with me every step of the way and I would be lost without him. As a small token of my gratitude, I will do my best to never let his name be forgotten again.

Until my relationship with Saint Jude, I was lost, wandering from house to house, job to job; always searching and never happy. What I wanted, what I needed, was twofold: a family and a purpose. Both have been given to me and for this I am eternally grateful. Realizing that my destiny lay not in a career or in money has been the greatest epiphany of my life. I was a tiny bug who, after years of struggling, had finally managed to make it through to the light. Illumination had finally come. It became clear to me what my true purpose was: to be a testament to Saint Jude Thaddeus and to introduce him to as many people as humanly possible. So that has become my mission, my life's work. I run the marina, yes, but it is the Jude Thaddeus Glen Cove Marina. It exists, like this story, for the purpose of furthering Saint Jude's shadowed name. As for family, well, I found that, too. In Saint Jude, I have found all the comfort, support, and love that any family could give. He is all the family I'll ever need. And lastly, I say this to you. Listen to your heart, listen to your faith, and embrace Saint Jude Thaddeus, the patron of impossible cases, the man who will one day no longer wear the name of the Forgotten Saint.